INTRODUCTION

The District of Bearsden and Mil[ngavie] [lies in the] valley of the rivers Allander and Kel[vin] [...] [...] [...] the Campsie Hills, some six miles to the north-west of Glasgow within Strathclyde Region.

Until 1975, Bearsden and Milngavie developed independently, with Milngavie becoming a Burgh in 1875 and Bearsden in 1958.

However, before these dates, both lay in the parish of Kilpatrick, and it is with the history of this parish, and the parish of New Kilpatrick in particular, with which this book is concerned.

Bearsden and Milngavie District was formed by the amalgamation of two Scottish Burghs in terms of the Local Government (Scotland) Act 1973, which was responsible for the total reform of local government in Scotland. Administration by the new District Council started on 16th May 1975.

One hundred years earlier, in 1875, the growth of the population in Milngavie was such that, in terms of the "General Police and Improvement (Scotland) Act 1862", it could be deemed to be a populous place and entitled to Burgh status, which was granted in May of that year. The first meeting of the new Council took place in what was part of the Milngavie Mechanics' Institute (established in 1836), known as the Bridge School, on 27th September 1875.

The first major change to affect the status of the Burgh occurred with the passing of the Local Government (Scotland) Act 1929 which entitled small Burghs, such as Milngavie, representation on Dumbarton County Council, as County Councils had become the authority responsible on a country-wide basis for functions such as education, public health and classified roads.

Bearsden, on the other hand, had a relatively short life as a Burgh, being formed in 1958 under the terms of the Local Government (Scotland) Act 1947. Seventeen years later, after a determined effort to maintain local independence which was carried out in association with the Burgh of Milngavie, these two Burghs now form part of the present Bearsden and Milngavie District, which is the smallest local authority within Strathclyde region, having a population of 41,000 now in 1994.

CONTENTS

GW01417327

PREHISTORY

All man's activities in the past have left traces, either by patterns in the land; the development of industry, or by the boundaries of government. Some of these patterns are obvious and are still to be seen many hundreds of years after the event. Some are less obvious.

Before the hand of man can be seen in the landscape of the district, the forces of nature imposed their own distinctive patterns on the landscape. The area to the north is bounded by the volcanic rocks of the Campsie Fells and the Kilpatrick Hills, which were formed during eruptions of lava some 335 million years ago. When volcanic activity ceased, the area gradually subsided and became a basin where sediments began to accumulate. At times this basin was submerged beneath the sea, and at times river deltas built out from the land mass to the north to change the style of deposition. A rich fauna inhabited the shallow tropical seas of Lower Carboniferous times, and when they died their skeletons became preserved in the mud on the sea floor, eventually becoming fossils when the mud became rock. There these fossils have remained until the present day – a fragmentary record of former life on earth. It is from these deposits that the Bearsden Shark (Stethacanthus) comes which was discovered in 1981. It was stated that there were at least 18 species of extinct fishes present in the Manse Burn, Bearsden, of which 5 belong to the shark family. Some of these fishes were known, but many were new and were indeed, unique to Bearsden. The best example is about three feet long, and behind its head, pointing skywards, is a structure like a giant shaving brush, the bristles of which are very large teeth and which look like nails. Also, there is an array of tooth-like denticles growing out of the forehead. Its mouth is at the front, inside the jaws of which are large teeth and at the back of the throat, a series of small teeth.

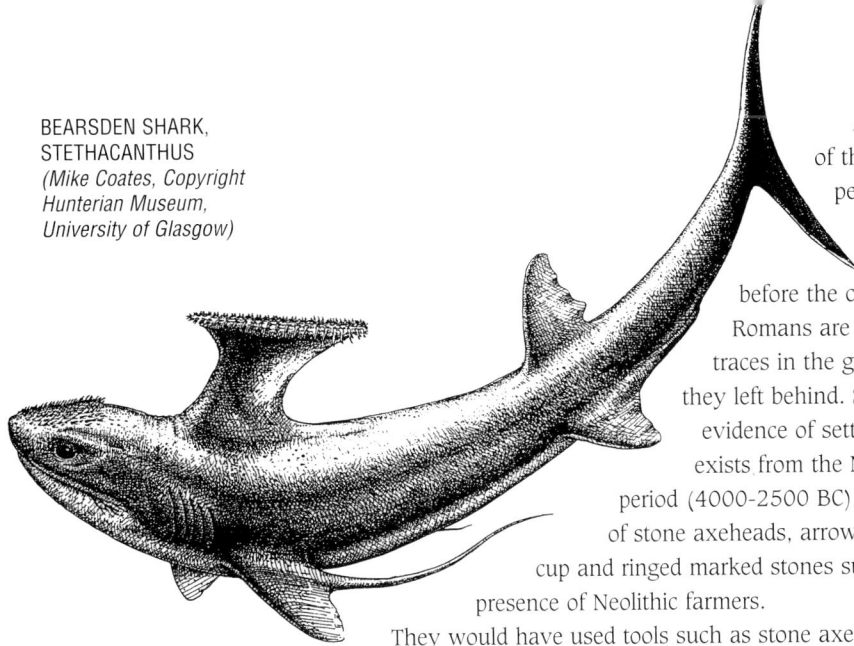

All we know of the prehistoric people who inhabited the District before the coming of the Romans are from the traces in the ground which they left behind. Some evidence of settlement exists from the Neolithic period (4000-2500 BC). Stray finds of stone axeheads, arrowheads, and cup and ringed marked stones suggest the presence of Neolithic farmers.

They would have used tools such as stone axeheads (c. 2800-2000 BC) found at New Kilpatrick, made of stone originally quarried in County Antrim or Rathlin Island, which were made by striking a lump of stone to drive off flakes until a roughly axe-shaped piece was obtained. Such axeheads would have been mounted in a wooden haft, held in place by natural resins and binding, and used for wood working, butchering, digging the ground, etc.

BRONZE AGE: 2500-500 BC

Around 2500 BC, a new culture came to Britain from Holland and the Rhineland. These first metal-using people were known as the Beaker people because of the very characteristic shape of their pottery. Bronze was used for tools, weapons and jewellery.

Several burial mounds, a stone axehammer and an urn containing human remains, along with flint arrowheads and bone beads, indicate that this area was part of a broad area of Bronze Age settlement centred on the estuary and lower valley of the Clyde.

A collared urn and its contents – namely four barbed and tanged flint arrowheads, a leaf-shaped flint arrowhead, four bone beads, mixed up with cremated human bone – were discovered around the turn of the century by workmen who were levelling the summit of the knoll at Mount Zion in preparation for the fourth and eleventh greens of Milngavie Golf Course. The material is about 3500 years old and is a particularly fine example of goods from a burial of that time. Artifacts associated with urn burials are relatively rare. Their presence here suggests that the corpse was wearing a necklace and probably a garment when cremated, and was accompanied by part or all of a set of archery equipment. The person's sex cannot be determined scientifically as the bones have disappeared, but by analogy with earlier Bronze Age burials it is likely that it is an adult male.

IRON AGE: 500 BC-400 AD

Around 500 BC, iron-using Celtic people moved into Scotland and mixed with the earlier inhabitants. Although few in number, they had great influence: they spoke a new language from which Gaelic developed, and they had built hill forts of stone and timber. It is possible that the raised area on which Mugdock Castle stands may have been a promontory fort, although there is no surface evidence to support this. By the 1st century AD, the area was occupied by the Damnonii, a Celtic tribe whose territory stretched over the area later identified with the Britons of Strathclyde.

THE AULD WIVES' LIFT
on Craigmaddie Muir

The Romans first arrived in Britain in 55 BC when Julius Caesar landed with a small expeditionary force. He was unable to advance due to lack of forces and bad weather, but returned in 54 BC when he was successful in overcoming the native forces before returning to the Continent.

Almost a century passed before a Roman army landed in Britain again. By 83 AD they had advanced into north-eastern Scotland under Agricola. A decisive battle at Mons Graupius was fought, but despite their victory, lack of manpower forced the Romans to fall back, and by 105 AD the new frontier was a line of forts from the Tyne to the Solway. The Emperor Hadrian visited Britain in 121 AD to inspect the frontier and instigated the construction of a linear barrier known as Hadrian's Wall. It runs from Newcastle to Bowness and is 73 miles long.

Following Hadrian's death in 138 AD, the new Emperor, Antoninus Pius, ordered the abandonment of the Hadrianic frontier and the reoccupation of southern Scotland. Once the Roman army reached the Forth-Clyde isthmus a new wall was built.

THE ROMANS

THE ANTONINE WALL

The new wall was built across the narrow waist of Scotland formed by the rivers Forth and Clyde. It ran for 40 Roman miles (60km) from Old Kilpatrick on the Clyde to modern Bo'ness on the Forth following, for most of its length, the southern slopes of the Central Valley of Scotland. This effectively brought the lowlands of Scotland within the Roman Empire and the Antonine Wall became its north-west frontier.

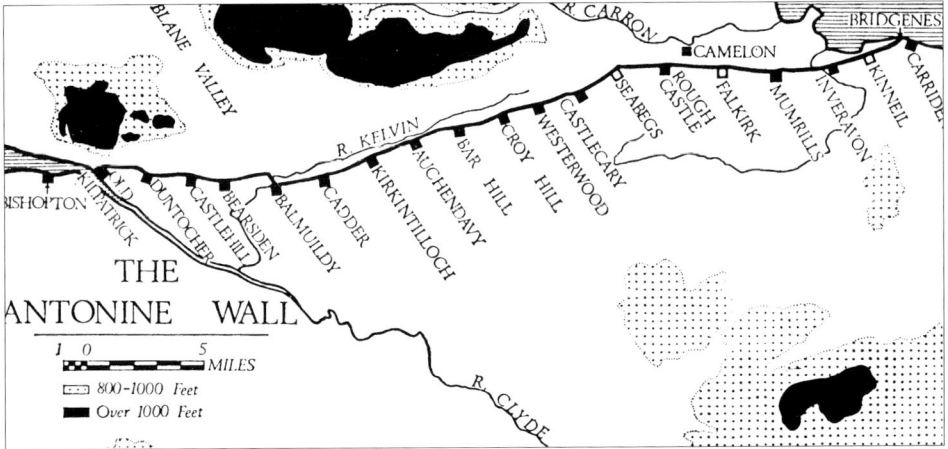

THE ANTONINE WALL

1   0   5
         MILES
800-1000 Feet
Over 1000 Feet

ANTONINE WALL:
Reproduced by kind permission of Glasgow Archæological Society

The actual building of the wall took place in several stages.

Firstly, the base of the Wall and the Military Way were constructed using large stones as a foundation.

Secondly, the rampart itself was constructed. This consisted of turf blocks stacked in layers to a height of 3-4 metres, above which was probably a wooden palisade and walkway.

Thirdly, the ditch was dug and the material deposited on the northern side to form an upcast mound. The Wall itself was built in sections starting in the east and the sections were allocated to the various legions involved in the construction work.

At intervals, usually of about 3.5 km along the Wall, were forts. There are thought to be 19 forts, of which 15 are known and 4 are suspected on grounds of spacing. In addition there are other minor installations – fortlets, signal platforms, civilian settlements, and construction camps.

Some of the forts were designed for a single regiment of 500-1000 men, others for smaller detachments and they were linked by a road, the Military Way. In between the forts lay fortlets, possibly garrisoned by 32 men. One fort lay at Bearsden.

The Antonine Wall was not an isolated frontier, as to the north a line of outpost forts provided a military presence up to the Tay, while to the south many forts were built along the main communication routes.

The Wall was not only a barrier. There were gateways through the Wall. Thus, people and goods could enter and leave the province, which was totally under the Roman control. The Wall provided a convenient demarcation line for the province within which Romanisation was encouraged.

Proof that the Wall was built in the reign of Antoninus Pius, when Lollius Urbicus was governor of the Roman province of Britannia, came, with the discovery in 1698, of the "Lollius Urbicus stone" at Balmuildy, just to the east of the modern boundaries of Bearsden.

Fortunately the Balmuildy stone and probably another stone, discovered at Castlehill, were acquired by the College of Glasgow. This was due to the lively interest taken by William Dunlop, Principal of the College 1690-1700, and by Robert Woodrow, college librarian 1697-1703. These men founded what became, in time, the collection of Roman stones, in the Hunterian Museum, University of Glasgow.

In 158 AD, the Antonine Wall was abandoned and the Roman forces withdrew south. However, they returned to Scotland almost immediately. The reason behind this evacuation is not clear. Possibly the Romans over-reacted to an outbreak of hostility in Northern England.

Although the Wall was reoccupied, there was a significant reduction in the size of the garrison throughout Scotland. Soon after the succession of a new Emperor, Marcus Aurelius, in 161 AD, the Antonine Wall was abandoned for good. War was threatening to break out in Britain and the main frontier reverted to Hadrian's Wall.

ANTONINE WALL:
New Kilpatrick Cemetery

7

In 208 AD the Emperor Septimus Severus carried out two campaigns in Scotland to restore peace, but after his death his son, Caracalla, when he became Emperor, ordered the Roman Army to withdraw from Scotland. After this withdrawal, they were never to reoccupy Scotland.

BEARSDEN FORT

Although noted by earlier antiquarians, the fort at Bearsden or New Kilpatrick, was not excavated until 1973 when the Department of the Environment were able to carry out excavations prior to the redevelopment of the site by Miller Homes Northern Ltd.

The fort itself covered 1 hectare (2·5 acres). It was attached to the rear of the Antonine Wall rampart, and defended by a rampart of turf on a stone base, and from one to three ditches. The fort was too small to hold a complete regiment but probably housed a detachment from the Fourth Cohort of Gauls, which was a mixed infantry and cavalry unit stationed at Castlehill, 2.4 km to the west.

Bearsden was provided with barrack blocks, stables, store-houses and a workshop all built of wood, two stone granaries, but no headquarter building and no commanding officer's house. The Military Way ran through the middle of the fort, forming the main street. "Roman Road" runs along the same line as this street.

The fort was abandoned and demolished by the Roman Army,

ROMAN FORT BATH HOUSE: *Antonine Wall, Bearsden*

probably in 158 AD, though the Antonine Wall as a whole does not appear to have been abandoned in favour of a return to Hadrian's Wall until about 163 AD.

THE BATH HOUSE

This building was provided for the use of all soldiers in the garrison. It lay a short distance from the east gate of the fort within a defended annexe.

The bath house was built of stone and timber – the heated rooms being of stone, owing to the risk of fire. The walls were plastered inside and out, with a special water-proof plaster being used on the inside. Some windows were glazed, and others protected by wooden shutters. The roof was either thatched or shingled.

The entrance to the bath house lay beside the fort rampart, and led into a large timber-built changing room. From here the bather passed into the cold room which was the central hall of the building. Here he was faced with a choice of bathing, either he could turn left into the hot dry room, continue on into the steam range or, turn right to the cold bath. The cold room contained a statuette of a goddess, probably Fortuna, the deity of bath houses, and an altar possibly also dedicated to Fortuna. When found, some walls and floors of the bathhouse still retained their original plaster, but exposure soon caused this to decay. In the cold bath, it was tried to simulate the Roman wall-plaster by a modern mix. Elsewhere, decayed Roman flagstones were replaced by modern ones.

The pillows supporting the floor of the second warm room and the hot room, were too decayed to expose, so they were buried in gravel for protection. To the north of the bathhouse, the walls of the early heated rooms, robbed by the Romans, were marked out in concrete, and a similar treatment was used to show the position of the destroyed south wall of the latrine.

A replica of the excavations was produced by the District Council for display at the Glasgow Garden Festival of 1988, and this replica may now be seen at the triangle formed by Milngavie Road and Strathblane Road, situated at Duncan's Garden Centre.

LATRINE BLOCK

The latrine lay south of the bath house, built against the inside face of the turf rampart of the annexe, with a gravel path leading to it from the entrance to the bath house. This was a communal latrine and would have contained seating for about 9 soldiers. The wooden seats were arranged over the shallow channel which ran round the side of the west and south walls. Water, led to the latrine through a network of drains, washed the sewage through the annexe rampart into the ditch.

Analysis of the sewage suggests that the soldiers had a diet of bread and barley, flavoured with coriander and opium poppy seed, figs, raspberries and strawberries, wild celery and hazel nuts. They would also have had meat, wine and beer.

DISTANCE SLABS

Along the line of the Antonine Wall, over the years, 20 legionary tablets or "distance slabs", set up by the Second Legion, and by detachments of the Sixth and Twentieth Legions, have been found. Each tablet recorded the length or distance of the Antonine Wall that had been completed by a certain working squad of legionnaires.

The distance slabs found from Castlehill to Old Kilpatrick recorded the completion of short lengths, measured in feet, while the distance slabs found to the east recorded the completion of long stretches each measured in Roman paces.

Apart from the Bridgeness slab, which marked the eastern end of the rampart and is now in Edinburgh's Royal Museum of Scotland, and the worn slab in Kelvingrove, almost all the other distance slabs can be found in Glasgow University's Hunterian Museum.

ROMAN POTTERY:
Antonine Wall, Bearsden

The slabs provide us with a fascinating insight into the Romans and their way of life, including their architecture, gods, ceremonies, clothes and emblems. Indeed, the slabs of the Second and Twentieth Legions often bear the legionary emblem – a wild boar in the case of the Twentieth and a Capricorn or Pegasus for the Second. Despite the fact that the "distance slabs" were concealed and buried as the Romans retreated from the Wall, all those centuries ago, their state of preservation is extremely fine indeed. And although in their present form, the slabs are quite dull and grey in appearance, there are indications that they could have been brightly decorated, in their original state.

The first confirmed journey made along the line of the Wall from the west coast to the east was by Alexander Gordon in 1723. Since then, many have trodden the same track, and no doubt will continue to attract archaeologists and explorers for many years to come.

Traditionally, the coming of Christianity into the area is linked with the name of Saint Patrick, after whom the parish is named. Kilpatrick means the "cell" or church of Patrick.

Little of solid historical fact is known about Patrick, but there is no doubt that sites associated with the saint were important centres of pilgrimage in the Middle Ages.

By around the Ninth Century, a recognisably Scottish church had emerged with Paisley Abbey, founded in 1169, becoming the ecclesiastical centre for the area.

The earliest mention of land ownership, in what is now the Milngavie and Bearsden area, was the dispute in the 13th century between Paisley Abbey and the Lennox family. The church of St Patrick was of particular significance as the supposed birthplace of St Patrick, and this is where the names Old and New Kilpatrick originated.

In 1227, Maldowen, Earl of Lennox, conveyed the church and its lands to the Monastery of Paisley. The land was much coveted and as J. Cameron Lees observes: "The wild Highlandmen, who inhabited that part of the Lennox, were continually seeking, by fair means and by foul, to obtain possession of them, and it took all the power of the church to hold its own against their devices".

Dugald, the Earl's brother, is listed as the "rector" of the parish at this time. He strongly resented and strenuously resisted the transference. Relations between the Lennoxes and the church continued to be strained as Dugald tried to exercise his right of ownership against that of the Abbot. As an educated man, in a period when only churchmen could read and write, he used his skills to forge charters which made him out to be proprietor of various local areas of land, including Cochmanach Dalevanoch, Bachan and Finbalach.

THE CHURCH

The seriousness of the case caused the Abbot in June 1232 to appeal to Rome, to Pope Gregory IX. The case was to be dealt with in Ayr and eventually, fearing excommunication, Dugald appeared before the appointed judges. Seeking mercy, he admitted his guilt, and thus was allowed to retain his church, but resigned the lands (which were not rightfully his anyway).

The parish remained until the Reformation under the supervision of the Abbot.

The discovery in Victorian times of a censer, known as the Bearsden Censer, points to the possibility of there having been a chapel in the Boclair area. But no further discoveries have been made which verify this. Nonetheless, the censer is rightly admired for its craftsmanship. It is thought to be eleventh or twelfth century in date.

The Reformation of 1560 ushered in a period of great difficulty for the parish church, and for a time services were conducted by lay-preachers. In 1575 the first post-Reformation fully ordained minister was appointed.

A key date in the church's history was the 16th of February 1649 when an Act in Favour of the "Ministers of Drumery and Kirkpatrick" was passed by the Scots Parliament. Its effect was to divide the Parish of Kilpatrick into Western and Eastern halves: Old and New Kilpatrick.

NEW KILPATRICK
PARISH CHURCH

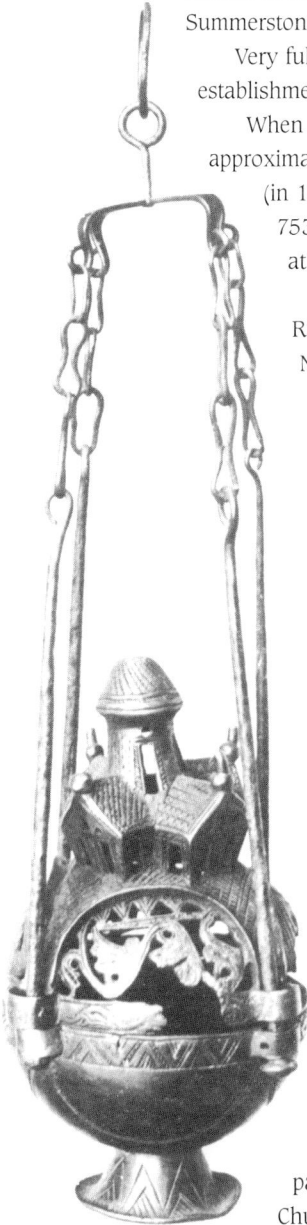

The area of New Kilpatrick in 1649 was 21 square miles and stretched from halfway between Duntocher and Whitehurst to Summerston, and beyond Hilton Park Golf Course to Yoker.

Very full records exist of church affairs, since the establishment of the Parish of New Kilpatrick.

When the parish was formed, the population was approximately 1000. It rose to 1700 (in 1791), to 10,815 (in 1891) and (in 1947) to 19,126: 11,596 in Bearsden and 7530 in Milngavie. Today the District's population stands at 41,000.

The earliest account of parish life was written by the Rev. George Sym in 1793 in which he called the parish New or East Kilpatrick. According to him, farming was the principal industry, but the land was "stubborn", manure was scarce and farmers were slow to try new methods.

In 1807, during the ministry of Mr. Sym, it was resolved to build a new church, which was opened for public worship on 21st February 1808. The architect was Mr James Stevenson, and it is interesting to note that the church cost £1605 and could seat 704 worshippers. The church was further enlarged in 1873, 1880, 1885 and 1910.

Dr Andrew Sym, who succeeded his father as parish minister, wrote a full and interesting account of life and work in New Kilpatrick in 1835.

Nowadays, to many people, Bearsden is synonymous with wealth. But it was not so in Dr Sym's day and still less so earlier. Dr Sym, it was said, know of only "six or seven resident families of independent fortune". And the fines imposed in New Kilpatrick from its very beginning were much lower than those of many other parishes, plainly pointing to the lowly circumstances of the people who lived there.

In Dr Sym's time, there were 3031 persons in the parish, of whom 1784 claimed connections with the Church of Scotland, 1104 with the Seceding Church, 112 with the Roman Catholic Church and 31 with the Episcopal Church.

Dr Sym was forced to report that neither his church nor the relief one at Milngavie was "as well attended as it ought to be". It was also thought that the religious character of some parishioners fell short of what is should have been. It seems that the residents' principal moral shortcoming was the "demon drink", and the existence of 18 licensed premises within the parish, or one for every 31 families, was not helpful.

New Kilpatrick's session Minute Books go back as far as 1693 with the exception of the years 1722-1782. In days gone by much of the session's time was taken up with "cases of discipline" such as Sunday-breaking, quarrelling, irregular marriages and sexual offences. For example, a Dougalston farmer who stacked his corn on Sunday, a Wester Clober man who took in his grain on a fast day, a Chapelton farmer who bartered some sheep for a cow on Sunday, and a Ledcameroch woman who left "the washing out on the Lord's Day" were all dealt with appropriately.

Violence of speech and action also came in for strong condemnation. In 1694 women from Chapelton and Lochbrae were summoned for "falling scandalously out" and "scolding and flyting".

The penalties exacted from offenders naturally depended on the gravity of the offence. Sometimes a warning would suffice, sometimes a monetary fine was imposed, and sometimes the culprits had to stand on the Stool of Repentance and make a public confession of their penitence.

Session minutes and records of births, marriages and deaths are substantially complete, and are housed in the national archives in Edinburgh.

With a rapidly increasing population in Victorian times, the need for new churches in the area became pressing. Initially the need was greatest in Milngavie with its flourishing bleach works, dye works and mills, and Milngavie Parish Church (later St Paul's) was opened in 1841. The present fine building came into use in 1906. Subsequent daughter churches of New Kilpatrick were Temple Parish Church (1892); Drumchapel Parish Church (1901); St Margaret's Knightswood (1932); Killermont Parish Church (1935), and Westerton Fairlie Memorial (1957). In the case of Westerton, religious services had been held in Westerton Hall, on the site now occupied by the library, since 1914.

The 19th century was also a time of disruption in the Church of Scotland with the Free Church breaking away in 1843. The first such

Top:
NORTH CHURCH
1900
Bottom:
SOUTH CHURCH
Prior 1941

"dissenting" congregation to be established in Bearsden was the New Kilpatrick United Presbyterian Church of 1874. It later became the South United Free Church, Bearsden, and from the Church Union of 1929, Bearsden South Parish Church. Bearsden Free Church (now Bearsden North Parish Church) followed in 1887. In Milngavie, Cairns Church traces its history back to the Kilpatrick Relief Church of 1799.

The old church, now swept away, was over 100 years old and occupied a site on the "Preaching Braes" overlooking the Tannoch Burn. In 1787, a petition to the Relief Presbytery of Glasgow for "pulpit supply" was made and granted.

The promoters of the movement immediately set about to build a church. However, its walls were just a few feet high when a hitch, relating to title deeds, caused the building to be abandoned. Undaunted, however, the supporters of the Relief in the New Kilpatrick selected another site at Hillfoot and began work there. All went according to plan here until the stonework was finished, when the "master of works" "condemned it" and the "Stickit Kirk" remained without a roof for 30 years. Hopes of a Relief Church for the "growing village" of Milngavie were fading fast when help came from an unexpected quarter.

Following a fire in 1795, at a large cotton factory at Deanston, Perthshire, many of the employees were discharged. As Milngavie was "home" to a similar mill, a number of the workers came to the Burgh. Having identified themselves as being "with" the Dissenters, the movement to build a church was revived. Steps were taken to complete the first building, when the efforts of the people were successful and the church was opened for worship in 1799. Later it became a UP and UF Church up to the time of church union in 1847.

St Lukes' began as Baldernock Free Church in 1843, transferring to Milngavie in 1894. St Luke's final move to its present building in Kirk Street allowed the former building to be purchased for the use of St Joseph's Roman Catholic congregation. The Episcopal Church in Scotland is represented in the area by two congregations, viz. All Saints, Bearsden, dating from 1897, and St Andrew's in Milngavie, which was built in 1892.

KILPATRICK
RELIEF CHURCH
Mugdock Road

A census of 1831 showed a total of only 19 Roman Catholic families in the parish, comprising 112 persons in all. From such a modest total, Roman Catholics have increased to two large congregations, St Andrew's in Bearsden (1967), and St Joseph's in Milngavie (1871).

In 1892 St Peter's College for the training of priests was opened at Courthill, Bearsden, and the college library was at first used as the chapel. In 1906, a new chapel was opened for the use both of the college and as a chapel. In 1946, however, a disastrous fire almost entirely destroyed the college and a new building was constructed in Cardross. This in turn was abandoned and the college transferred to Newlands, Glasgow, before finally returning to Chesters House in Bearsden in 1986. The college is run on an inter-diocesan basis and was renamed Chesters College and now Scotus College, which houses a small but fascinating museum.

No account of the church life of Bearsden and Milngavie would be complete without mention of some smaller – but no less active or dedicated – congregations. The oldest of these, with just over a century of existence, is the Allander Evangelical Church in Milngavie. The United Free Church in Milngavie dates from 1929, while more recent are the Baptist Churches in Bearsden (1973), and Milngavie (1985), and the Bearsden Full Gospel Fellowship. Although members of the Society of Friends (Quakers) had long attended services in Glasgow, it was only in 1983 that a local meeting was established.

CAIRNS CHURCH, MILNGAVIE
Buchanan Street and Cairns Drive Junction

The recorded ecclesiastical history of the area spans a period of over 800 years and embraces almost every major denomination, in addition to smaller independent groups. It is a record of almost continuous growth, and it has also produced artifacts of great interest and beauty.

THE LAND

After the departure of the Romans, the area was left to the warring tribes of Scots, a Gaelic-speaking people from the North of Ireland, and the Britons, who occupied the Lowlands of Scotland. The area bounded by Strathblane and the Allander Water, by Craigallion in the west, and Kilsyth in the east, contains many ancient burial grounds and must have been home to a large, scattered community and would have been part of what became the Kingdom of Strathclyde under the control of the Britons.

It was ruled in St Patrick's day (389-461 AD) by Coroticus, a Briton who was denounced by the Saint for slave raidings in Ireland. St Ninian, and to a greater extent St Mungo, brought Christianity to Strathclyde in the 6th century, but after the death of the latter saint in the early 7th century, the area relapsed into anarchy. Mugdock may perhaps be identified, although there is no archeological evidence, with Magedauc or Maesedauc, mentioned in the Welsh Chronicles, as the place where a battle took place between the Britons and the Picts in c.750 AD and it was here that King Talorgan of the Picts was killed. Among many speculations as to the origins of the stones known as "The Auld Wives Lifts" on Craigmaddie Moor, one is that they were set up to commemorate this particular battle and although most authorities are inclined to regard the "lifts" as a natural formation and date the carved pagan head symbols rather earlier that the 8th century. The "Gowk stane" above Strathblane is also associated with this battle.

It was not until the time of Malcolm III that religion and some order came to be imposed upon the land. As times improved, a feudal state evolved under the Canmore lineage, especially during the reign of David I (1124-1153). This was based on the English pattern and the relation of vassal and superior. The superiors were the Anglo-Norman barons who came to live in Scotland and were given land by the King.

And so it was, that in the 12th century, great areas of land came to be held by powerful families. The Lennox or Levenachs was just such a family.

The Barony of Lennox included Dunbartonshire and the Parishes of Fintry, Kilsyth, Campsie, Strathblane, Baldernock, Balfron, Drymen and Inchcalleoch (Buchanan). Alwyn, the first Earl of Lennox, is said to have been a Saxon who fled from Norman domination in England.

About this time, the church, which was of great importance as the religious power, was placed on a firm basis. Each Baron formally granted a tenth (tithe) of the value of his land and their produce to a church, founded on, or built on the land. Land so tithed became a Parish and thus the Parish of Kilpatrick was created out of part of the huge Lennox Barony.

DIVISION OF LENNOX ESTATES

Early in the 13th century, three large Baronies were created from the Lennox lands in our area.

The Barony of Drumry was associated with the captaincy of Dumbarton Castle. It passed through Galbraith hands to the Livingstones.

Bardowie was given by Maldowen, the 3rd Earl of Lennox, to Maurice, first of the Galbraiths. The name Galbraith may be derived from Gaul Briton (or Welsh speaker), a north Clyde variant of the Welch or Wallace found south of the river. The Galbraiths became a notable Stirlingshire family. In 1296 "Arthur de Galbrait" was one of the principal Barons who swore fealty to Edward I. They served their senior Earl (Lennox) well and later were given additional lands at Balvie Mains and Garscadden. Their first manor place was Craigmaddie Castle, which in 1550 was given up in favour of Bardowie. Along with their lands, the Galbraiths were given the power to try and punish miscreants and if it came to hanging, the Earl of Lennox's only stipulation was that is should be done properly and on his gallows, at Mugdock on the knowe, near Craigend.

The Galbraith line came to an end with three heiresses. In 1373, Janet Galbraith married Nicholas Douglas, who thus acquired Mains. And about the same time, a second Galbraith daughter married a Logan, taking with her the lands of Balvie. The Logans of Balvie ended in the 17th century when Humphrey Colquhoun acquired the lands of Balvie which in 1770, was sold to Robert Campbell. Once again in 1819 they changed hands when they were acquired by James MacNair, who remained in possession until 1839. Mains House, built on the site of Balvie House, was occupied until 1954 by the Douglas family.

At the end of the 13th century, Malcolm, the 4th Earl of Lennox gave land to Sir Patrick de Graham, ancestor of the Dukes of Montrose. These lands were not erected into a Barony until 1458. A good case is made, by some authorities, for equating the name Graham with Grime or Grim (meaning devil), rather than with the Norman, "De Grahame". The Barony included the lands of Garscube, Killermont and Kilmardinny and from Balmore in the east to Dumbarton Muir in the west, a great crescent of land from modern Stirling District, through part of Strathkelvin District, Bearsden and Clydebank to Dumbarton. The manor place was Mugdock Castle. The Grahams found it inconvenient to have their lands partly in Stirlingshire and partly in Dunbartonshire and asked that all should lie in Stirlingshire. In 1388, Robert II, King of Scots, gave his approval for this transfer, and it was not until 1891 that Milngavie returned to Dunbartonshire.

Mugdock Castle was a Graham stronghold until around 1700, and it was there that the Grahams held court and had their prison.

Sir Patrick Graham died at the battle of Dunbar in 1296 fighting against the English for the independence of Scotland. His brother, Sir John Graham, the friend of Sir William Wallace, was killed at the Battle of Falkirk in 1298.

Sir David Graham was taken prisoner at the Battle of Durham of 1346, along with King David II. The oldest surviving part of the castle was probably built by him or his father, David, who died in 1329. William, 3rd Lord Graham and 1st Earl of Montrose, fell at the Battle of Flodden in 1513.

Robert, Lord Graham, eldest son of William and 2nd Earl of Montrose, fell fighting for his country at the Battle of Pinkie in 1547.

Because of the famous exploits of many of its members, the family was known as the "Gallant Grahams". The family motto is "n'obliez" (forget not).

The most famous member of the family was James, 5th Earl of Montrose, who was later known as the Great Marquis.

Other members included John Graham of Claverhouse, Viscount Dundee, last upholder of the ill-fated cause of James VII in Scotland, and who died at the Battle of Killiecrankie in 1689.

Another member was Thomas Graham, Lord Lynedoch, a hero of the Napoleonic Wars.

The family was elevated to the Dukedom in 1707.

THE GREAT MARQUIS
1612-1650

James, 5th Earl of Montrose was born in 1612 and was educated in Glasgow and also at the University of St Andrews. He was 14 when his father died and two years later he married Magdalene Carnegie by whom he had two sons. Following her death in 1633, he spent 3 years on the continent. Upon his return, he actively supported the Covenanting Party under the Marquis of Argyll, with whom he had a series of famous victories, including the defeat of the Royalists at Newburn in 1640.

Montrose was the first member of the Privy Council to sign the National Covenant in 1638. Later, disillusioned with the leaders of the Covenant, he joined the King's Party (Charles I) and was subsequently arrested and imprisoned in Edinburgh. On his release, he returned to Mugdock, but in 1643 was commissioned Lieutenant General for King Charles in Scotland and created a Marquis is 1644.

Again he showed his skills in a series of Royalist victories but his army was surprised and totally defeated at Philiphaugh in 1645. He fled to the continent but returned after Charles I's execution to join forces with Charles II. In 1650 he was betrayed and taken prisoner, and on 21st May 1650 he was hanged, drawn and quartered at the Cross in Edinburgh. His head was placed over the gate of the prison and his arms and legs sent to Glasgow and the other main towns, to be displayed over their gates. After the Restoration of Charles II, his remains were buried in state in St Giles Cathedral.

Although the "staitly house of Mugdock" was partly destroyed on Parliament's order in 1641, James Graham returned to live there in 1644. In his absence on campaign, the Laird of Buchanan was ordered to attack the castle and remove "all the gaites and windowes". Mugdock Castle was subsequently forfeited to the Marquis of Argyll. When it was returned to the Grahams in 1655, the house was uninhabitable and took two years to rebuild but was "a poor dwelling for a Marquis".

However, at that time, the status of Mugdock was raised considerably as it was able to hold a market every Friday, and a free fair in August and November.

MUGDOCK CASTLE AND ESTATE

Mugdock Castle stands on a promontory which falls steeply on the north and west but has a gradual approach on the east and south. The latter sides were probably protected by the loch and ditch. Mugdock Castle is the most interesting mediaeval fortress now surviving in Stirlingshire after Stirling Castle itself. Together with the castles at Tantallon and St Andrews, it is amongst the most important examples of its period in Scotland.

The earliest reference to a castle in Mugdock is in 1372. The castle was built around a courtyard which was entered through a gatehouse with portcullis. All that remains is a high stone wall with towers on the north-west and south-west corners.

After the beginning of the 18th century, Mugdock declined in importance and Buchanan old house replaced it as the principal residence of the Graham family. The last Graham left Mugdock c.1840 and Mugdock was then occupied by numerous other tenants until the Duke of Montrose finally sold the estate and Castle to the family of Sir Hugh Fraser in 1945. It was last occupied in 1948.

Mugdock was gifted to Central Regional Council by Sir Hugh Fraser in 1981 for use as a Country Park.

JAMES GUTHRIE SMITH
1834-1894

Smith was a well-known local antiquarian whose family had links with Craigend. He leased Mugdock Castle in 1876, demolished the earlier house in the Castle courtyard replacing it with a large mansion in the Scottish Baronial style. He also built stables and offices in the outer courtyard as well as altering and repairing the older castle buildings. Most of the mansion however was demolished in 1967.

Further Division of the BARONIES OF BARDOWIE & MUGDOCK

Opposite Page:
MUGDOCK CASTLE
S.W. Tower and portion of adjoining Curtain Wall from N.E. 1958

Dougalston was possibly first recorded in 1232 as the residence of Dougald, son of the 2nd Earl of Lennox. It remained in the hands of the Grahams for many generations. John Graham built a new house in 1707. Dougalston was sold in 1767 to the Glasgow merchant, John Glassford. John Glassford was the first identifiable commuter. From the Kirk Session records it would appear that, although living in the Parish and proposing to join New Kilpatrick Church, he still retained his connection with his Glasgow business. He died in 1783 and his son, Henry, sold Dougalston to Robert Ker, early last century. A new house was built and survived into the the 20th century, but in 1839 it was said to be in a neglected state of repair. The Dougalston mansion and policies were offered to Glasgow Corporation as a home for the Burrell

Collection in the 1950s. However, on account of the National Coal Board activities in the area, Dougalston was not thought suitable, and was returned to the Connell Trustees. The estate became the property of the Stakis family in the 1960's and today part of it is in use as a golf course.

Clober remained for many generations in the hands of the Grahams. In 1773, James McGrigor, a Glasgow merchant, was granted a long lease of the house and grounds by the Duke of Montrose. Later Robert Dunlop acquired the lease and added to the house. Alex Dunlop, an Edinburgh advocate, was proprietor of the property in 1875. Clober House, which was a handsome building, was finally demolished in the 1960s to make way for the Crawford Road housing development. The names McGrigor, Watt and Dunlop have been given to local streets.

The lands of Boclair are first mentioned in the 1388 Mugdock transfer. The name Boclair would seem to show that cattle rearing has a long history in the District. "Bo" could be derived from Gaelic, Latin or French for "ox" and "clare" or "claire" can also be traced to the purpose or condition of tenure of land. Eventually the Boclair estate was divided into Boclair and Temple of Boclair. The proportioner was one William Mitchell, who divided the land between two heiresses, but unfortunately his love affair with one of the women came to light and he was excommunicated by the Presbytery and imprisoned in Mugdock Castle on December 27, 1696.

Killermont estate was mentioned among the Mugdock lands about the end of the 13th century. It is referred to in the 1630 Valuation, and about this time it was in the possession of the Cunninghams of Drumquhassil but in 1628 John Cunningham sold Killermont to John Stark. About 1680 the land was again sold, this time to James Hunter of Muirhouse. In 1747, it was bought by Lawrence Colquhoun, whose father owned Garscadden. His daughter, Agnes, inherited Killermont and married a John Coates Campbell. They had a son, Archibald, who assumed the name Colquhoun on succeeding his mother in Killermont, and also inheriting Garscadden. Archibald became Sheriff of Perthshire and Lord Advocate. He had two sons, the elder John Campbell Colquhoun, succeeded to Killermont and Garscadden.

The modern house, still standing today, was built about 1800. In 1901, Mr Sinclair of Glasgow Golf Club, began negotiations with the laird of Killermont for the Golf Club. Eventually, the son, A. J. Campbell Colquhoun, agreed to a 20-year lease at £400 per year rental and

£1000 compensation to the farmer. Thus the Glasgow Golf Club acquired its present course and club house. At 1pm on May 21st 1904, Sir John Ure Primrose, Lord Provost of Glasgow, opened the new course by driving off from the first tee.

When the Galbraith family, Barons of Bardowie, was left with three heiresses in the 14th century, Garscadden estate passed to the Flemmings of Biggar and later to Robert Erskine. In 1655, it was acquired by William Colquhoun, writer in Glasgow. The Colquhouns gave distinguished service in the senate, at the bar and in literary pursuits. In 1832, the owner of Garscadden, John Colquhoun, a distinguished scholar, was returned to Parliament for the County of Dumbarton. All traces of the fine Garscadden House and Mill have disappeared.

Mains estate was acquired by the Douglas family, through marriage, to one of the three Galbraith heiresses, Janet. The Douglases were the second oldest family in the District at the time and were destined to play an important role in Scottish history. When the intrigues between Roman Catholics and Protestants were at their height in 1571, Mathew Douglas, 5th Laird of Mains, seized Dumbarton Castle for the King of Scots. Later his son, Malcolm Douglas, was beheaded at Edinburgh Cross along with his father-in-law, for his alleged part in the Gowrie conspiracy and raid on Ruthven. Chief witness against him was Edmonstone of Duntreath, near Strathblane. Later Edmonstone admitted he had made up the evidence to save himself. The "manor site" of the Douglases of Mains was at what is now known as Old Mains. This survived until about 30 years ago, when it was demolished to accommodate Douglas Academy in Milngavie.

Early last century, John Campbell Douglas, laird of Mains, gave up his old house and moved to Balvie House which he purchased and renamed Mains. Balvie House no longer exists but appears to have stood just off the Stockiemuir Road to the east and north of Crossburn. The Logans had acquired Balvie from the Galbraiths, by marriage, and held it for many generations. In 1526, John Logan of Balvie and his son, Walter, were accused of murdering their neighbour, John Hamilton of Bardowie and his son, John. About 100 years later, Balvie was acquired by Humphrey, second son of Sir Alexander Colquhoun of Luss.

A certain John Colquhoun married Lilias Graham of Mugdock, and abducted her sister, Catherine. He was accused of using witchcraft to persuade the girl to go with him. He was sentenced to death but succeeded in escaping and apparently was never executed. In 1700, Balvie was sold to Robert Campbell, an Edinburgh lawyer, and later became incorporated into the Dougalston estate and finally it was acquired by John Campbell Douglas, and renamed Mains House.

Craigmaddie or the rock of God (Gaelic) is a small property which was part of the Barony of Bardowie and has a castle, of which part of a tower still stands. This was at one time a stronghold of the Galbraiths of Baldernock. For a time the lands were in the hands of the Hamiltons and then became part of the Dougalston estate. The manor house, still standing, was built by James Black, Lord Provost of Glasgow, about the end of the 18th century. Towards the end of the last century, the owner was Major Graham Stirling, who commanded the 42nd Regiment during the Crimea War.

Craigend originated as a farm on the Mugdock estate and was formerly called Gallow Knowe since it includes the small hill on which the Lennox gallows stood. The land passed from the Lennoxes to the Grahams and in 1660 to Robert Smith who was grandfather of John Smith who began the booksellers business, which still bears his name in Glasgow. In 1851, the Smiths sold out to Sir Andrew Buchanan who was British Ambassador at the Court of Vienna. Later the property passed to Yarrows the shipbuilders. For a time, from 1949, Craigend housed a zoo but as it was too far from public transport, it failed. The Craigend lands are now, in part, incorporated into the Mugdock Country Park. The old house is now in ruins but the stable block has been reconstructed as an attractive Visitors' Centre for the Country Park.

Kilmardinny went, in part, to Sir John Colquhoun "under the Great Seal" in 1465 and the Colquhouns kept the land for many generations to the beginning of the 18th century. After the Colquhouns, Kilmardinny became the property of the Grahams of Dougalston. When the family lines ended, the estate was purchased by Rev. Andrew Gray, parish minister of New Kilpatrick, about 1730. He was presented to the parish by his patron, James, Duke of Montrose, but his appointment was not popular and it was only with great difficulty that he was accepted. Following the Grays, the house was occupied by several Glasgow merchants. Kilmardinny House and the loch area were acquired by the former Bearsden Town Council in 1965 from Sir John McDonald, a Glasgow builder. The house is now used as a centre for the performing arts. The loch is a sanctuary for some rare water birds.

Garscube or Garscoob, to give it an older name, was among lands given to Umphredus de Kilpatrick by Maldowen, Earl of Lennox, about 1250 but the Colquhouns appeared to have owned the land until the reign of King Charles II, when it was acquired by John Campbell of Succoth, who was legal adviser to his unfortunate kinsman, Archibald, Earl of Argyll and was present with him on the scaffold at his execution. His son married a very beautiful woman, Helen Wallace, who died at Garscube in 1767. Their son became Lord President of the Court of Session in 1789, and Lord Rector of Glasgow University in 1799. He died at Garscube in 1823, aged 89. The last Garscube House, a very fine building of sandstone, was built in 1827. The estate was acquired for Glasgow University after the last war, by Sir William Wyper, the eminent head of the veterinary school who was first to use X-rays on animals. The estate now houses the University Veterinary School, research unit, a hall of residence, and the West of Scotland Science Park in which the University co-operates with industry. Garscube House was demolished in 1955.

AGRICULTURE

It is probable that our prehistoric ancestors cleared areas of the land both by burning, and with stone axes, in order to grow wheat and barley. Animals, such as cattle, goats, sheep and pigs would also be domesticated.

The earliest reference to agriculture in the district is in a court case of 1220 concerning the endowment of the lands of Old Kilpatrick to Paisley Abbey. Mention is made of a man who sheltered some people in his cottage at Thombulthe or Tambowie but was later murdered during a cattle stealing raid.

From the 14th century, records improved and names of farms start to appear in recognisable form, eg, Gartconnel, Mains, Balvie, Bonnaughton, and Baljaffray.

In medieval times the land would be worked by small groups of peasants owing dues in kind, or labour, to their superiors.

Life for these peasants was very hard. Houses were mostly of twigs and clay, the one room being shared with cattle for warmth as there would be a central fireplace with a hole in the roof. Crops were unpredictable and a bad harvest meant considerable suffering.

The Rev. David Ure's 1794 survey of agriculture in Dunbartonshire and a study of rent books, showed three classes of farm workers. The lowest were the poffelers and pendicle holders. A poffle was

MOSSHEAD FARM

simply a small plot of land and a pendicle was a piece of land "appended to an office or duty", or granted as an inducement to a tradesman or craftsman to settle in the district. This name survives in Bearsden's Pendicle Road. These farm folk worked minimal amounts of land for bare subsistence. The middle group were tenants for the lawyer and merchant lairds and they often paid considerable rent but had access to lime and manure. Lastly were the lairds themselves, who let parks and surrounding mansions for grazing or fattening cattle. These were the cause of many complaints until the end of the droving times. Dunbartonshire landowners had a bad name for not allowing stopping places, and fencing the droves in. Thus cattle were driven without rest through the county, with consequent loss of weight or condition.

Below the three classes of "farmers" were the "servitors and servitrices", the farmhands who were the last to benefit from any improvements. According to the survey, the only relief for these workers was when an Act of the early 18th century made a cash payment rather than statutory labour, for work on the roads.

In 1699, Lord Belhaven suggested improvements in the design and layout of farm buildings which involved the separation of people from animals, and the building of proper chimneys.

Many local farms have stones dated between 1790-1800 indicating that progress was slow.

A good layout positioned the house in the centre, with dairy on one side and byre on the other. The fourth side was often stables with men's quarters above.

As the 19th century progressed, workers' cottages tended to be a little apart for the "steading". The radical nature of the changes brought about by the Agriculture Revolution since the latter part of the 18th century has destroyed much of the evidence of the early improved farm building.

Tenure has also changed over the years. Scottish Feudal Tenure has been described as a jungle into which only the brave would venture. It seems that at one time the peasant had so many duties to various superiors that he had little time to tend his own land. All his crops had to be processed at the landlord's mill. Tenure was usually for 19 years in the late 18th century. From time to time, at least two or three years' rent had to be written off on account of bad harvests. Rent books describe the practice of "kain or reek hens". This meant that in addition to rent, each tenant farmer had to hand over one of more hens for every "lum reeking" on his holding. Sometimes the gamekeeper had to be given broody hens for pheasant rearing. These impositions were much resented.

Without post and wire fencing, it was not easy to keep cattle out of growing crop fields. When the Galbraith estate of Gartconnel was divided in the 14th century, they also received holdings on Cameron Moor, near Finnich Toll. These were probably for summer grazings (sheilings) away from the crops. New Kilpatrick always seems to have been a fairly prosperous farming area, perhaps because the soil and climate were good. Dunbartonshire was well placed to attract successful lawyers and merchants from Glasgow.

The opening of the "Great" Forth-Clyde canal and, later, the development of railways opened up transport to markets. By 1860, there were over 100 farms and at least 20 businesses related to farming in the parish. Some farms are now golf courses, riding schools, garden centres and even the Veterinary School at Garscube. At the end of the 18th century, there was a considerable increase in the interest of agricultural improvements. New crops were introduced, land was enclosed in fields and farmers began to organise themselves in producing, for example, ploughing matches. Farming included crop cultivation and animal husbandry. Among root crops, turnips were grown but were less satisfactory than potatoes, which were sold in

PLOUGHMAN & HORSES
Thorn Farm, Bearsden

Glasgow. Carts taking potatoes to the city returned with loads of horse manure, in the same sacks! Oats, wheat, barley and rye were also grown as major crops and rotated on a six-year cycle. An average sized farm of £30 rent per year would have one plough. In the 1870's, there would be about 50 farms of this size in the parish. Larger farms paying £200 rent might have had two ploughs with three or four horses kept to pull them. An average farm of 100 acres (40 hectares) might have had 12 milk cows each producing about 4.5 litres of milk and about 0.5 kg of butter per day, for seven months of the year.

Highland Black cattle were sold for about £2:10s each in 1790. They were fattened up on good grazing land and sold for twice that amount to butchers.

Flax was also an important crop, and the development of flax growing stimulated the establishment of the Milngavie Linen Factory which brought a number of looms into one complex with an overseer.

From old maps, session records and valuation rolls, Bearsden and Milngavie Historical Society has been able to trace over 100 farms in the District, 19 of which are still working. Of these, 12 are over 300 years old, 6 are over 100 years old, and one is at least 100 years old.

All around Milngavie there were farms which are now no longer in existence. On the north side, there were Barrachan and Craigholm. Moving down Mugdock Road there was a farm at Drumclog Avenue.

Nearer Milngavie there was a farm at Cheapside opposite where the Red Cross Hall now stands. Cows from this farm were driven through the Cross every day to graze in the fields where Clober Road and Ferguson Avenue now are. Clober Farm is now the Golf Club. Millbrae Farm stretched from the station to Braehead Avenue. Mosshead and Burnbrae farm lands have been covered with houses and Kilmardinny is now not even a riding school. Keystone Farm became a rugby field, garden centre and police station. Crossveggate, now built over, extended from Baldernock Road to Fairways and included Lennox Park.

A small farm at Kersland, opposite the lane, had a gate at the back. Cows climbed the hill and grazed where Glassford Street and Garwhitter Drive now are. Barloch Farm was off Strathblane Road near the water tower.

Milngavie was a busy market town, with the market situated at the corner of Sinclair and Woodlands Streets. There were pens and loading ramps at the station, allowing the railway to take sheep and cattle to their new homes. A slaughter house stood at a site near Lennox Park. The streets became very dirty with the movement of cattle and horses from McAulay's stables where Homebrae House now stands.

The first farm machinery appeared 100 years ago. These were binders to cut and tie the grain into sheaves and were pulled by three horses. Sheaves were set up to dry and built into haystacks rather like big round tents. The stacks were then thatched to keep them dry. Some farms had round thrashing mills driven by water wheels or horses walking around. Thus grain was separated from straw. If the grain was too wet for threshing it would be taken to the corn mill where there was a kiln for drying. Oatmeal was popular for human consumption; other grain was crushed to a large extent to feed the cattle, pigs and hens. The farms produced a lot of milk and there were dairies in Strathblane Road (Allander), Mugdock Road (Co-op), Douglas Street (Mrs Brown's), and Main Street (Mrs Watts). Potatoes were transported in large amounts by rail to Glasgow. Dung for fertilizer came back by rail from the Glasgow streets, and much lime was produced locally.

Due to the fact that there were so many horses, blacksmiths were busy. Two of the largest forges were situated at McAulay's and McConnel's in Station Road (now the Lillie Art Gallery).

DISCOVERING BEARSDEN & MILNGAVIE

REMAINS TO BE SEEN

KEY:

- 🟠 Farms In Use
- 🟩 Old Industrial Sites
- ⊕ Archaeological Sites
- 🔴 Water Grain Mills
- ⬟ Tolls
- ᎍᎍᎍ Antonine Wall

ALLANDER WATER

MUGDOCK

AULD WIVES LIFTS

MUGDOCK RES.

CRAIGMADDIE RES.

CRAIGMADDIE BURN

CRAIGDHU BURN

MILNGAVIE

BARDOWIE LOCH

MANSE BURN

CASTLE HILL

ANTONINE WALL

ALLANDER WATER

ROMAN BATH HOUSE

BEARSDEN

CANNIESBURN TOLL

RIVER KELVIN

FORTH & CLYDE CANAL

Milngavie itself has always been the only village of any significance in the modern Bearsden and Milngavie District. The first map reference to "Milgay" appears in the work entitled "The Lennox", of the cartographer Timothy Pont in 1654. "Milnegai and the Milne and coalheughs of Milnegai" are mentioned in earlier charters and retours and also in an Act of Parliament of 1649. It seems to have been part of the land of Caistone or Gaistoune, Anglicised to Keystone about 60 years ago. The village appears again in Richardson's map of 1795 which shows Milngavie as an important feature on east-west and north-south routes, with a bridge over the Allander. The level of the Allander still rises and falls rapidly, and after heavy rain would be almost impassable without a bridge. The first ordnance survey map of 1851 shows Milngavie as a village of some considerable size. In the case of Bearsden there are only a few large villas between the tiny hamlet near New Kilpatrick Church and the Canniesburn Toll with its ancient smithy.

WESTERTON GARDEN SUBURB

On August 16, 1912, the Glasgow Garden Suburb Tenants Ltd was registered under the Industrial and Provident Societies Act and the garden suburb movement in Scotland was born.

Until the suburb was established, the management was undertaken by a number of influential people, among them Sir John Stirling Maxwell LLD and Sir Samuel Chisholm LLD. The aim of the co-partnership movement was to make the interest in houses not individual but collective, by giving the householder a stake in its self-government, thus stimulating communal interest and public spirit.

The site for the Glasgow Garden Suburb was selected on the Garscube estate. The land was more than 250 feet above sea level and commanded an extended view of the Kilpatrick Hills and Campsie Fells. An option was taken on about 200 acres of land obtained at £15 per acre feu value, which at 20 year purchase was £300 capital value per acre; £60,000 capital value for the 200 acres. The superior constructed a road connecting the suburb with the western boundary of Glasgow at a cost of £200, but all other expenses of the development were borne by the society.

In May 1911 the North British Railway Co. received a letter from the society informing them of the proposals. It was thought then that eventually the development would house 300 families but the letter pointed out "the proposal depends entirely on whether or not a station is built".

By November 13, 1912, after many months of patient negotiating between the management committee and railway company, work had started on building a station at a total cost estimated about £3368.

The station opened for coaching goods and mineral traffic on August 1, 1913, with "Westerton Garden Suburb" on the name boards.

On May 24 that year, the first tenants had moved into their new homes. The first 60 houses were complete early in 1914. In 1915, 84 of the houses were occupied, but by this time the war and the cessation of government had stopped further progress in building.

Today Glasgow's Garden Suburb at Westerton does not stand alone, surrounded by nothing but green and fertile fields. Now, the surrounding area is a built-up residential zone. On June 5th 1987 the Westerton Garden Suburb houses were designated as a Conservation Area by Bearsden and Milngavie District Council.

Prior to the 1914 war, housing development in the main was by private enterprise. After the war it was realised that many of the older houses did not comply with required standards and that planning of the Burgh of Milngavie was necessary. In the years between the wars, the Burgh Council built 350 houses. The 1939 war stopped developments but after the war, up until 1975, the Burgh built a record number of 1200 houses including the "prefabs" at Cloberfield. These "aluminium houses" helped to accommodate people who lost their homes in the Clydebank "blitz", by the German bombers in 1941. On the site of the old Ellangowan Paper Mill on the banks of the Allander, houses were built including a sheltered housing element for senior citizens in Mugdock Road. Land for private house building was and still is in demand in other parts of the district.

The revolution in transportation during the last two centuries has been one of the major factors shaping the development of Milngavie and Bearsden. In the mid-18th century the small market town of Milngavie was served by a motley collection of tracks and roads. Bearsden, as yet, hardly existed. However, improved communications were to attract population, stimulate industry and produce a largely suburban area.

The Forth and Clyde canal, passing through the south of New Kilpatrick parish and completed in 1790, was an obvious stimulus to trade and transport. For example, coal from the Temple coal-works and stones from Garscube quarry could be carried, and farmers near the canal could use it to carry materials, such as dung, transported from Greenock. However, according to the Statistical Account of 1845, "heavy duties meant it was not all that less expensive than carting materials from Glasgow".

Perhaps of more significance to the area was the improvement in roads associated with the introduction of turnpikes. Tolls were set up and the money raised was used to maintain the roads. Allander and Canniesburn Tolls developed in this manner. Tolls were levied as late as 1883. Stage coaches ran daily between Milngavie and Glasgow. It was carriages that carried the hand loom weavers, used as strike-breakers, from Glasgow to the Milngavie Printfield during the calico-printers' strike of 1834. Improved roads also stimulated industrial growth. Cloth, for example, could be carried more easily to and from the numerous bleachworks of the area. By the mid-19th century it was therefore claimed that "the want of good roads . . . has been long since remedied, the parish being intersected in every direction with turnpike or other roads, the former of which are in excellent condition".

However, the coming of the railways was to have the most profound impact on the area. By the mid-

TRANSPORT

KILLERMONT
TERMINUS

19th century Glasgow had the highest density of population in western Europe. Areas such as Hillhead and Kelvinside were still seen as suburbia. The next half-century saw the expansion outwards of the city and its suburbs – the arteries of growth were undoubtedly the railways.

In 1863 a single-track line to Milngavie was completed by the Glasgow and Milngavie Junction Railway. "The district was lightly populated, but prospects of early development as a high-class residential area had motivated its sponsors". A station was built on the line at what was called "Bearsden".

HORSE BUS
Drymen Road

By 1896 the North British Railway Company, which had taken over, decided to double the line and reconstruct Milngavie station. This was the result of an ever-growing demand for the railways. In 1884 there were 13 trains to and from Milngavie each day. By 1896 this had risen to 24 each day. Passengers in the 1890s pressed for more services in order to facilitate shopping, concert and theatre visits to Glasgow. Concern felt by the North British about tramway competition and

BEARSDEN STATION
1903

possible competition from the Caledonian Railway prompted the building of Hillfoot station at the turn of the century.

Bearsden and Milngavie had obvious attractions. They were "just distant enough from the city to escape its smoke and other contaminations; but not too far away to be difficult of access". Social segregation became more apparent. Before, merchants had lived in close proximity to the working classes in the city. Now, they were able to live in a more salubrious environment in a distinctive residential area. It was reported in 1902 that over the previous three decades in Bearsden, over "350 villas and cottages have been erected" as well as "large terraces and blocks of buildings with splendid shops and many handsome public buildings". Bearsden had grown unrecognisably into "a large and fashionable suburb" of over 3000 inhabitants.

The railways also served industry. From the 1890's branch lines went to the Dye Works at Burnbrae and the Ellangowan Paper Mill. In more modern times, changes have included electrification in 1959/60 and the recent de-manning of many stations on the line. For the moment, Milngavie station remains manned thanks to its being the end of the line.

The most recent change has been the partial single-tracking of the line.

One of the major rivals of the railways was that most nostalgic form of transport – the tramways. Glasgow had the second largest tram system in Britain, and in 1906 Glasgow Corporation extended its tram lines to Killermont. For almost 30 years, proposals were put forward to extend the line to Milngavie. Two plebiscites were held, in 1907 and 1913, in Milngavie. In 1907, 491 voted for the extension, 240 were against. Six years later the vote was still in favour but the majority was down to 103. However there were various delays. The tramways were faced with rivalry from the railways and buses, and there was some

NO.29 MILNGAVIE
TRAMCAR

reluctance to see Glasgow Corporation extend its powers beyond the city boundaries, so the progress of the line was gradual. By 1922 it had reached Canniesburn, and a year later it terminated at Hillfoot.

Eventually the line to Milngavie was opened to great popular enthusiasm, in October 1934. The first service was between Milngavie and Mount Florida (red cars, service No.13), the maximum fare being 2½d. This was soon followed by a service between Milngavie and the Renfrew Ferry (blue car, service No.14). After 1945 two other destinations went to Broomhouse and to Gairbraid Avenue. However, by the mid-1950s the era of the tram was beginning to draw to a close – the Milngavie line ended in 1956.

The mid-1950s also saw the removal of one of the most amazing sights in Milngavie – the Bennie Railplane. In the 1920s, the Scottish inventor, George Bennie, patented his design for a revolutionary new form of transportation, a cross between a railway and an aeroplane. The Railplane was designed to complement, not substitute for, the railways. It was to carry passengers and perishables or light goods, while the railways carried heavier and bulkier freight. Bennie believed that the Railplane could run suspended from an overhead structure above existing railways. The Railplane was seen as a solution to the traffic problems of the age, as well as a means of providing employment in an era of economic depression.

Tests formally began on 8th July 1930 above the LNER line running to the Burnbrae Dye Works in Milngavie. A steel super-structure, over 400 feet long, was constructed. On it ran the full-size Railplane car, cigar-shaped, made of aluminium alloy and driven by propellors at each end. At first the car was powered by two 60 hp petrol engines. Bennie hoped that ultimately it would travel at 120 mph. The size of the track limited a full testing of speeds and braking, although it did reach up to 50 mph. The highest speeds were reached in 1931 when new electric motors were fitted. Inside, the car was luxurious and could carry up to 50 passengers.

Yet, for the next 25 years the Railplane lay rusting at Milngavie. Bennie never lost confidence in his system – he tried to develop it in England, Ireland, the USA and the Middle East. Perhaps its very novelty hindered its development. Its early years unfortunately coincided with the great depression, when few wanted to take a gamble, and later, all forms of transport had to compete with the increasingly popular motor car.

INDUSTRY

The origins of industry in the District are linked to the plentiful supply of water from small streams as well as the river Allander. The streams were a source of power used to turn water wheels. It is probable that there was a water-powered grain mill in Milngavie before the time of James IV (1488-1512).

Timothy Pont's map, published by Blaeu in Amsterdam in 1654, shows Milgay with a mill and a bridge over the Allander. At that time, Milngavie would have been a tiny place with no real industry other than milling.

By 1791 Milngavie, with a population of 200, was "the only considerable village in the Parish of New Kilpatrick."

Bearsden, at that time called Kirktoune, New Kirk or New Kilpatrick, was only a tiny hamlet with a few houses round the Parish Church. By the end of the 18th century, there were four oat mills, two barley mills, and a snuff mill using water power provided by local streams. There were also several smiddies, including one at Canniesburn Toll.

In the 18th century, the flax or linen industry was, apart from agriculture, the most important source of employment and income in Scotland.

A linen mill, the "Milngavie Factory", was set up in the 1740s and was in production until c.1754.

By the beginning of the 19th century, the improvement to roads, and the completion of the Forth and Clyde Canal, improved communications and stimulated industrial growth. The coming of the railways continued this development and was responsible for the growth of both Bearsden and Milngavie.

In Milngavie, the textile industries expanded with, by 1790, a cotton mill at a site now occupied by the Community Education Centre and Library; calico (cotton) print works in Clober Crescent in the south side of the present-day Station Road and also at Crossburn. A Turkey Red Company dyeworks was established about 1840 near the site of the Burnbrae Hotel.

The bleaching industry played an important part in the textile industry, as it was necessary to treat the raw materials – cotton and linen thread – in order to rid it of coloured impurities and to make it white. Bleaching was carried out at Craigton, Craigallian Loch and Clober.

Other industries which developed in the 19th century were a paper mill, first in 1790, at a site behind the shop, Iceland, then at the disused cotton mill site in 1870, which became the Ellangowan Paper Company.

The connection with paper was continued with the establishment in 1951 of James Ritchie's, later Bowater Containers (Scotland) Ltd., on a new site at Cloberfield Industrial Estate.

The West of Scotland Laundry started in 1882, first in Main Street, then in Clober Road.

Aerated water or "ginger" was being manufactured in Milngavie by 1860 and continues to the present day, with James Garvie and Sons factory near the site of the old paper mill.

Whisky was distilled at Tambowie from 1780 until the 1920s.

From these beginnings, industry has diversified into a number of smaller businesses mainly situated on the modern industrial estates at Cloberfield, Riverside and Crossveggate.

Interestingly, the earlier industries of cotton spinning and papermaking are to some extent continued today with Flexible Ducting and Bowater.

The provision of power by water has now given way to that provided by gas and electricity.

A private gas works was built by John Learmont in 1851 near the War Memorial in Milngavie. Bearsden houses were served with gas by the Partick, Hillhead and Maryhill Gas Company.

The Strathclyde Electrical Supply Company, later the South of Scotland Electricity Board, and now Scottish Power first installed electricity in the District in what was Scotland's first "garden suburb" in 1913 in Westerton.

Although some coal was mined at Baljaffray, and possibly at Langfaulds, it is unlikely that it would have been burned for domestic use, but used for burning lime.

Modern industry may rely for its power on different sources, but is still sited in the District close to the river and water supplies which originally gave it birth.

OLD GAS WORKS
AT MILNGAVIE
(Now Memorial Gardens)

LINEN

The flax or linen industry was during the 18th century, apart from agriculture, the most important source of employment and income in Scotland. Growth increased even after cotton was introduced at the end of the century. A linen mill, the "Milngavie Factory", was set up in the 1740s. A partner in the firm was John Graham of Dougalston and an overseer was appointed "to control the weavers". The mill lay on the Allander, and in 1745 consisted of 21 looms with accommodation for more and a commodious house for the overseer. There were lodgings in the village for weavers and a good bleachfield. The company was sold in 1750 and its fate after 1754 is not known, nor is the exact site of the mill. The significance of the factory was that it attempted to bring a considerable number of weavers together under one roof with an overseer to supervise the workforce. Prior to this it is likely that the local linen industry had been a cottage industry. There is also evidence of the existence of a flax rotting pound at Tambowie. Flax was left in such pounds to allow the soft tissues to rot, leaving the strong cellulose fibres intact. Rotten flax was then "dressed" or "heckled" which involved the repeated drawing or combing of the stems of rotten flax over beds of nails by hand, until finally only the linen fibres remained.

PRINTING

In the late 18th century, Parish Church records showed printers and "pencillers" of cloth among church members in Milngavie. In 1790 wooden block printing was first introduced by Walter Weir for calico (cotton) printing at works in Clober Crescent which is situated on the south side of Station Road today. In 1826, John Black and Company took over from Mr Weir. The printing industry up till then had been in financial trouble, but under the Blacks it began to prosper. There is a record that the highly successful and prosperous Glasgow merchant, James Glassford of Dougalston, renewed the lease of the printfield in 1835, and a relative, Henry Gordon Glassford, again renewed the lease in 1864. The ordnance survey map of the 1860s confirms that the site of the printfield was near the railway station. Homes for the printworkers were built on the east side of Strathblane Road in the "New Town". The printworks were finally demolished in 1901.

The COTTON MILL

A cotton spinning mill was established in Milngavie in 1790 by James Donaldson and Co. The site, where Milngavie Library now stands, was a feu on the farm of Cloberhaugh, granted by Henry Glassford of Dougalston. In 1795, the mill grew in size with the arrival of workers from Deanston in Perthshire, whose own mill had been destroyed by fire. The new arrivals about 100, were housed in what was called Highland Row, now partly covered by Garvie's soft drinks factory. Later, in 1825, the mill passed into the hands of Cappel and McKerrel and in 1839 the owners were Robert McGregor and Co. who employed 200 men, women, and children. The working conditions were 12 hours per day for five days, and nine hours on Saturdays, with child labour much in demand. In his account of the parish, written by the Minister, Mr J.T. Peat, we learn that in 1866 the Parish Church of the time in the centre of Milngavie, rang its bell to wake the mill workers at 5am. With the American Civil War (1861-1865), supplies of cotton became scarce and work at the mill declined.

BLEACHING

Bleachers were no doubt attracted to the Milngavie area by the abundant supplies of soft, mud-free water. The softness of the water would effect a great saving in the cost of soap used. Care was taken to keep the bleachfields mud-free by forbidding the ploughing of neighbouring fields and the watering of cattle in the streams.

There were old bleachfields on the west bank of Craigallian Loch. In fact, the flat stones, to which the cloth was attached, can still be

CRAIGTON BLEACH WORKS

seen, between the loch and the West Highland Way. The Blackwoods, an old Milngavie family, bleached cloth at Craigallian but gave up working there in 1831 when the water became too muddy.

Prior to 1760, bleaching was carried out in a small way by Allan Park at Clober or Clochbar (meaning "the path to the stone") at a site on the Allander, opposite the junction of Stable Road and Cloberfield. It is recorded that in 1763 Graham of Dougalston granted ground to James McGrigor at Clober for bleaching. In 1775, McGrigor's daughter married James Watt, the 29-year-old Greenock-born engineer, who developed the steam engine. Later Watt helped his father-in-law to extend and modernise the Clober Bleachworks. He laid out new water-ways and installed a boiler and machinery. His suggestion of using chlorine water for bleaching was followed, and it seems probable that Milngavie was one of the first to use chlorine for bleaching. There are records that cloth came from Holland – such was the reputation of the Clober Bleachworks.

However, the oldest bleachworks in the vicinity were probably at Craigton – a small community which sat 1½ miles above Milngavie.

Back in the 13th century, Craigton was part of the great Earldom of Lennox. After changing ownership several times over the centuries, in 1787 Sir Islay Campbell, an advocate and landlord, granted part of Craigton to James Robertson merchant of Anderston, Glasgow, and John Hunter, bleacher of Stockingfield, Glasgow, for bleaching for 60 years at £80 per year for 20 years and at £100 per year for the rest of the lease. These were large sums 200 years ago and indicate the

profits which would be made from the bleaching industry. In 1805 Archibald, Lord Succoth, agreed to pay £150 per annum for the site for the rest of the lease. In 1815 James Dunlop acquired Craigton House and the bleachworks, and in 1831 William Blackwood and Sons gave up bleaching at Craigallian and moved to Craigton.
The Blackwood family remained there until 1926.

Horses for the bleachworks' carts were stabled at Craigtonhill Farm. Loads of material to be bleached or after bleaching were carried by packmen. In 1921 a steam-driven lorry (Foden) was acquired by the Blackwoods. It is interesting to note that Craigton, isolated in the country as it was, appears to have thrived for nearly two centuries, especially as one of the greatest advantages of chemical bleaching was that works could move into town. To appreciate why Craigton remained the centre for bleaching for so long, one has to consider the Craigton community as a whole. By the mid-19th century, it was a thriving community with a smithy, farm, distillery, quarry and of course the bleachworks. A school was built about 1906. It was described as a pleasant place in which to live. It was a compact, independent place, fairly contemptuous of its larger neighbour, Milngavie. Stockiemuir Road, on which Craigton stands, was a turnpike, but nonetheless a pretty rough track, and within living memory the road-man would fill in potholes with turfs taken from neighbouring fields.

At times up to 60 people were employed at the Craigton bleachworks, working from 6am until 6pm, six days a week. Some girls walked the 1½ miles from Milngavie, daily. Others came over the slopes of the Kilpatrick Hills by the old footpath from Hardgate, a much longer journey. No doubt they were often late and were eventually put up during the week, in the "Wuman Hoos" at the bleachworks.

Coal for boiler fuel, sometimes in a form known as "gum" or dross, washed from larger pieces, was brought by cart six miles from the Forth and Clyde canal at Temple and from the Milngavie railway goods yard.

It appears that cotton yarn and possibly thread, but not cloth, were bleached at Craigton. The terms, cops, warps, lanks and faps, appear frequently in the works accounts. These were attached to chains with tally marks to identify customers' material. The tangled material left attached to the chains were used by children at Craigton School when they were learning to knit.

The chains, carrying the material to be bleached, passed slowly through tanks of boiling solutions of caustic soda, taking six hours in passage. They were then sprayed with bleaching liquor, followed by vitriol and finally, exhaustively washed. Colour was sometimes added to the wash tubs to produce light blues or pinks. Chains then passed through a "storing house". The drying stove was installed about 1849 by the Blackwoods along with a 60-ft chimney stack. The builders' estimate for the work came to £486:7s:3d.

In 1926 John Blackwood gave up bleaching at Craigton and went to stay at Clober House, near where Crawford Road is now located. The Blackwoods' similar works at Springfield in Glasgow were also closed and the business was concentrated under the Bleachers' Association of Manchester, at a factory in Barrhead. The machinery at Craigton was quickly disposed of. However, some senior bleach workers at Craigton were determined not to give up. In particular, a George B. Forbes, who had been book keeper, also a S. N. Shivelton, the manager, and an R. Fleming, were all convinced that bleaching could continue.

With £5,000 raised from Milngavie acquaintances, the Craigton Bleaching Company, with a registered office at 5 Glenside Crescent (Station Road), Milngavie, was set up in 1927. Cotton yarns were accepted for bleaching from Lancashire spinners. Hanks of cotton went to explosive factories as material to bind time fuses. Bandage cloth was produced from gauze, which was sent to Craigton for purifications, bleaching, and packing in bales, before forwarding to hospitals. Fine shirting material was made by D. and J. Anderson from thread bleached at Craigton.

The works obviously had a good reputation and as a result the new company prospered. Eight new cottages were built for workers in 1938 with other workers coming daily on foot from Milngavie.

Early in the Second World War (1939-1945) the Board of Trade closed the bleachworks, which were, however, kept on a care and maintenance basis. Finally in the late 1940s, the Craigton Bleaching Company went into voluntary liquidation and all shareholders were paid in full.

The WEST of SCOTLAND LAUNDRY

The old laundry, as it was called, was started in 1882 by Robert Learmont and Joseph K. Fairlie (Provost of Milngavie, 1901) at a site now occupied by the Scout Hall in the Main Street. The business prospered and new premises were built in Clober Road, just south of its junction with Craigton Road. The new building on the east side of Clober Road contained "the most up-to-date machinery for the rapid production of immaculate linen" and came to be regarded as one of the best-equipped laundries in Scotland. Sixteen shops in Glasgow acted as receiving centres. At one time 200 people were employed at the laundry, making it one of the main employers in the town.

After the 1939-1945 war, commercial laundry work declined with the advance of washing machines. The laundry buildings were, for a while, occupied by the Gymnastic Equipment Company. Modern flats were later built on the laundry site and a car repair workshop occupied the stables. During the building of the flats, trouble with the foundations was experienced when the builders uncovered an old well. This was at one time used as a source of water by the laundry when the Allander water was low.

DYEING

A Turkey Red Company's dyeworks was established in the area about 1840. It stood on both sides of Milngavie Road, near the site of the Burnbrae Hotel. Turkey Red was a bright and remarkably "fast" (permanent) dye brought to this country from Turkey at the end of the 18th century. The dyeing process was very slow, taking weeks and involving many steps. The dye had no affinity for vegetables (cotton, linen) nor animal (wood, silk) fibres. And so the cloth had to be treated so that the dye would stick. The agent is known as a mordant (biter) and it also determined the final colour produced. The improved procedures of M. Papillon, a French dyer, were brought to Glasgow in 1795 and used in the dyeworks of Hendry Monteith and Co. But despite the improvements, dyeing still took from 24 to 30 days to complete, using Turkey Red. Dyers were usually unemployed during the winter, since their work involved spreading cloth or yarn to the elements in the summer. In 1854, an English chemist, W. H. Perkins, produced the first completely synthetic "aniline" dye. This revolutionised the dyeing industry and by 1875 the old processes were largely abandoned. Presumably the new dyes were used at Burnbrae since dyeing continued there until the 1914-1918 war.

The PAPER MILL

A paper mill was started in Milngavie in 1790 and later employed 22 men and some women in the hand production of 20 reams (400 sheets) of paper a day. Following the installation of new machinery, 15 men and 15 women were able to produce 600 reams a day. The site of this mill, and its fate, before the appearance of White's Mill on the abandoned cotton mill site, are not clear.

About 1870 William White, a Glasgow rag merchant, converted the disused cotton mill for paper make-up. Nine years later it was purchased by John Gray, who later failed. In 1882 it was sold by public auction for £8,500 to the Ellangowan Paper Company. The sole partner at the start was Col. John Birrell. However, later, Andrew N. Bertram became a partner and the firm enjoyed considerable prosperity. In 1887 a second paper-making machine was added, and the Ellangowan Mill came to be regarded as one of the most up-to-date paper mills in the country, specialising in the production of high quality writing and printing paper suitable for book work and cheque books. After the 1914-1918 war, work was diversified with the production of paper for the Glasgow cigarette factories.

Boiler fuel was brought by horse and cart to the mill from barges on the Forth and Clyde canal at Blairdardie. Spent lime from the pulp digesters, where grass was treated, was loaded on wagons and pulled by Clydesdale horses with hooves protected by sacking. The grey-white mixture of earth and lime can still be seen.

In 1944 some excitement was caused by a fire, thought to have started spontaneously in the grass store. The "grass boiler" house was destroyed, but units of the National Fire Service saved the main buildings. The company had been trading in liquidation for some years and in 1944 all interests were acquired by Mr A. I. Macnaughton, a chemical engineer, and as a result the paper manufacture was put on a new footing. Five years later the mill was sold to the Clyde Paper Company which operated for a further 10 years.

CLYDE PAPER CO.

51

PAPER PRODUCTS

In 1850, 19-year-old Andrew Ritchie married 17-year-old Christine Walker in Glasgow and persuaded her to help him to make paper boxes for sale. Boxes were much in demand at the time and were made by hand, using paper, a scoring knife, shears and a pot of paste. The Ritchies' home and workshop were in the city and they worked hard six days a week. After five years the couple moved to Brunswick Street to be nearer their customers. In 1874, son Andrew was taken into the business and then James was born. In 1888 the factory moved for the third time, and 14-year-old James was working a 60-hour week, making boxes. By the end of the century, the Ritchies' Candleriggs factory occupied two floors and employed scores of workers. In 1915, James Ritchie visited the USA and was attracted by the new corrugated or rucked paper boxes. Eleven years later, James Ritchie returned to the States and placed an order for $200,000 worth of machinery, a vast expenditure for the time.

A plant was built at Bridgeton to produce 200 feet (61m) of corrugated paper a minute. The first Scottish paper corrugator was operating here in 1929. Sir James Ritchie, who by now stayed in Craigmillar, Milngavie, merged the company in 1944, with Eburite Corrugated Containers Ltd. Soon it became necessary to look for a larger manufacturing site – where better than Milngavie? The business was transferred in 1951 with considerable increases in plant and machinery, and the company became a part of the Bowater organisation. When Ritchies came to Milngavie in 1951, the total output of corrugated paper board was 20 miles per week. At the 25th anniversary of Bowater Containers, Milngavie, this had risen to 250 miles per week and the number of boxes had risen from 100,000 a week to one million. By 1987 Bowaters were employing 245 people in Milngavie at their plant in Cloberfield Industrial Estate.

MILNGAVIE – ITS RADICAL PAST

Milngavie, before its growth into suburban status, had a tradition of economic unrest and radical agitation. This had much to do with the industrial basis of bleachworks, calico printing, and textiles.

Industrialisation in Scotland brought with it cycles of economic distress. One such depression precipitated the so-called "Radical War" of 1820. The post-Napoleonic era saw large-scale unemployment among artisans. Demands for wider political rights were met with repressive legislation. Throughout central Scotland industrial unrest saw many mills and factories closing down. On April 1st, a poster went up in towns and villages calling for a provisional government. Radical supporters drilled and awaited a call for action in many towns. In the "Glasgow Herald" in April it was reported that 400-500 people were drilling in Milngavie awaiting the call to march to Glasgow. Hussars and Yeomanry were dispatched.

Five prisoners, guns and ammunition were taken. Most radicals were expecting the visit, and hearing no call to march, had fled. Two men from Milngavie cotton mill were charged with treason. It was claimed that they had posted the address of 1st April in Milngavie. The men protested that they had been handed the poster by a stranger, an *agent provocateur*, without realising its significance. However, the only confrontation was a relatively minor affair at Bonnymuir in Stirlingshire and as a result the Radical cause fizzed out.

Unrest continued to boil in Milngavie and in May and June 1820, a strike took place at the cotton mill, over wage rates. In June a few of the workers, mainly women and children, returned to the mill. Reports in newspapers stated that some of the strikers, in frustration, fired guns into the houses of the "black legs". They were arrested and charged with illegal combination and intimidation. The jury, however, found the verdict "Not proven".

Events died down at the mill until in September two men tried, unsuccessfully, to set the mill on fire.

CALICO PRINTERS' STRIKE OF 1834

The growth of industry, chiefly bleaching and calico printing, in Milngavie, was associated with the development in industrial and political radicalism among the working population.

The best example of this was the calico printers' strike of 1834. The strike grew out of the printers' complaint about the employers' practice of paying different wage rates for the same quantity and quality of work. The dispute came to a head in the late part of 1833. Strikes broke out in most printing areas in the west of Scotland. The printers were supported by a well-organised union.

In Milngavie, the strike began in November 1833 and was mainly associated with the Milngavie Printfield, run by John Black and Co (situated near the present railway station). This was the largest works in the area, with 130 block-printers as well as bleachers and dyers.

By January, 1834, rumours circulated that new hands were to be taken on. The strikers organised patrols to watch all entries to the village. In February the employers did take on new hands, mostly hand loom weavers, in an attempt to break the strike. Twenty-five of the new hands were to come to Milngavie on the third of February, escorted by 12 hired constables.

On their arrival, it was reported that a crowd of 500 had gathered outside the works and missiles were thrown. The works were then broken into and the weavers were removed from the premises and were marched into Glasgow.

The strike, however, was ultimately unsuccessful due to the fact that union funds became exhausted, and poverty amongst the strikers hit Milngavie shopkeepers. Soldiers escorted the new hands back to Milngavie, and they were billeted in the village. Arrests were made and some of the strikers were imprisoned. An atmosphere of suspicion and threatening violence hung over the village for the next few months.

AERATED WATER

Various forms of aerated water or "ginger" to give it a popular generic name have, for over a century, been manufactured in Milngavie. In 1860, George Milne had a factory at No18 Douglas Street, behind the Iceland shop. The site was known as "Ginger Hill". Later, Alex Strathdee acquired the business and used the name "Allander Springs". He had several other activities including farming, quarrying, and running a public house.

In 1929, the well-known modern firm of James Garvie and Sons Ltd acquired the Ginger Hill Factory. Shortly afterwards they moved to No52 Main Street, at the tram terminus, just before the Black Bull.

Ten years later, they made an important change in production, moving from "swing stopper" to "crown cap" bottles, no doubt facilitating manufacture with new machinery, but the new bottles were much more difficult to open. Ideally, they required an "opener" although a few boys claimed that teeth could be used to remove the cap.

Even at the end of last century, the need for a good supply of pure clean water, for the "drinks industry", was appreciated and the local aerated water industry has had the advantage of water from the Burncrooks Reservoir.

In 1959, Garvies started building a new factory on the site of Allander House. This house had been the home of Col. Birrell, a former owner of the paper mill, which had stood nearby. Buildings were added on the north side in 1963 and 1969, the last one partly covering Highland Row. The total aerated water works is now in excess of 65,000 square feet, making Garvies one of the largest soft drinks manufacturers in Scotland. A large variety of high quality soft drinks, squashes and syphons of soda are now produced and distributed.

The present plant includes a bottle-washing machine, which can remove old screw caps which are not re-used. Concentrates, made up to secret recipes, are prepared in an upstairs "syrup" room and fed by gravity into bottles. Soda water, a solution of carbon dioxide gas, under pressure, is added. This and capping and labelling are done automatically.

WORKERS AT
TAMBOWIE DISTILLERY

DISTILLING

Tambowie, which could mean "Tam's Bothy", dates from 1160 and is part of the community of Craigton, lying on the Stockiemuir Road. A distillery was founded next to the farm in 1780 and employed five men. The water was said to be of a particularly good quality. Barley from Morayshire was used exclusively and the fires for the stills were fuelled by peat from Tambowie Moss. A fine single malt whisky was produced viz 48,000 gallons of it in 1885. Occasionally the Church ministers would hint that too much of the local spirit was drunk in the parish's many hostelries.

In 1824 the distillery was let to Alex Graham, owner of Tambowie Farm, who remained there until 1884. He was followed by David Chrystal and in 1889 by Alex Ferguson, who handed over to Alex McNab in 1891. He remained in charge until 1920. A few years earlier, buildings had been destroyed by a serious fire and as a result the works closed. A horse-drawn fire engine came from Clydebank to fight the blaze. The manager ordered large casks, full of whisky, to be broken open in case they exploded.

Legend has it that men came from Milngavie with bowls and pails to collect the precious liquid as it flowed away. Some were said to have been found days later in ditches and under hedges rather the worse of wear.

POTTERY

Hugh "Ugolin" Allan worked briefly as a potter in Milngavie from 1904 to 1908. Born in 1862, the eighth child of a Glasgow builder, he studied at the Glasgow School of Art and adopted the name "Ugolin" to distinguish himself from a rival of similar name. He became well-known as an accomplished artist in oils, watercolours, tempera and black and white illustration. And in 1902 he turned to pottery. Although living in Glasgow's Charing Cross, he decided to set up his pottery in Milngavie. And while it is not certain of the exact where-abouts of his studio, it is thought it could have been in the old laundry building where the Scout Halls in Main Street now stand. His friend, Robert MacLaurin, an industrial chemist, who lived at 13 Claremont Gardens, helped to set up the pottery and to keep the coal-fired kiln going. However, Allan's health was not good and he died at the early age of 47. Allanderware, which is very scarce, is simple and attractive. The potter was self taught and threw his own pots. Several examples of his work are on display at Glasgow's Kelvingrove Art Gallery.

MILNGAVIE WATER-WORKS

Undoubtedly the most beautiful man-made feature in Milngavie is its water-works. Completed over a century ago, its walkways and well cared for gardens have attracted visitors from near and far. Indeed, when the trams were running from Glasgow to Milngavie, a visit to the water-works was part of the summer holiday at "the Fair" for many families.

It was on September 5, 1850, that Glasgow Town Council, acting for a population of 333,657 appointed a committee "to consider the city's water supply and to report on measures for its improvement".

The Council was urged to get its water from Loch Katrine, in an ambitious and far-sighted scheme. Predictably the scheme presented to the Council in December met with immediate opposition. However it was approved on December 27 by a majority, and was then promoted to Parliament.

Among the opposition was one Fred Penny, professor of chemistry at the Andersonian University of Glasgow who, surprisingly ahead of his time, said that the action of the soft water on lead piping would render it extremely hazardous to the health of the people. Other equally eminent chemists said there was no risk, and it took over 100 years to prove that Penny was right, before lead was replaced by plastic piping.

The preamble of the Bill failed, having cost £11,094:10s:10d. However, in August 1854, the Glasgow Town Council returned to the struggle. Famous engineers Robert Stephenson (Menai Bridge) and Brunel (Great Western Railway) confirmed the suitability of Loch Katrine. The Bill went before the Commons in April 1855 and received Royal Assent on July 2, 1855.

The water level at Loch Katrine was 367 feet above sea level and that of the proposed service reservoir at Milngavie 317 feet: high enough to give good service to almost all points within the Glasgow boundary. A 25¾ mile long aqueduct was required, some of it tunnelled through hard rock, and was to be 8 feet in diameter. A reservoir was to be constructed near Mugdock Castle, which would have a surface area of 62 acres, would be 50 feet deep and would hold 550 million gallons of water, viz 11 days supply. The water was of such high quality that at first only straining through fine copper wires was called for.

Work on the water system began in the spring of 1856 and was completed in 1859. Queen Victoria travelled from Balmoral via

Holyrood Palace and Callander to Loch Katrine arriving on October 15. The Royal party sailed on the "Rob Roy" to the mouth of the tunnel where the Queen turned a handle to admit water to the aqueduct. In March 1860 city dwellers began tasting the new water.

The total cost of the work was £924,141. All in all it was a remarkable piece of Victorian engineering, completed on time and within budget.

The Mugdock reservoir dam was built by large numbers of Irish labourers and is popularly known as the "Micky dam". These Irish workers were housed in tenements on either side of Mugdock Road, near Sinclair Street.

Construction of a second water supply was authorised by Act of Parliament in 1885. The aqueduct was to be 23½ miles long, between Loch Katrine and the new Craigmaddie Reservoir adjacent to Mugdock Reservoir at Milngavie. This project took considerably longer than the first and was not completed until 1896. The Loch Katrine water supply is augmented by water from Loch Arklet (1914) and Glen Finglas Reservoir (1965). The 1855 scheme provides 45 million gallons per day to Mugdock reservoir, the 1885 scheme 80 million gallons per day to Craigmaddie reservoir. Thereafter, water is discharged into five 36-inch diameter pipes from Mugdock and the same from Craigmaddie, for the Glasgow area. Modern developments have been the additions of chlorine to the water for sterilisation. More recently lime is added as a slurry with water using 20-ton lime silos, and like the chlorine is automatically monitored. The lime makes the water less acid and thus less likely to dissolve lead which is injurious to health. Also in recent years a high count of viruses in the water was blamed on seagulls resting on the water. So bird alarm calls were broadcast from vans to scare the gulls away, and the viral counts have since dropped.

The water industry, nowadays, is highly technical and requires skilled manpower. The complex from Loch Katrine to Milngavie is run on a day-to-day basis by a great number of Water Department employees. Some work at Milngavie monitoring flow rates, acidity and chlorine. Surprisingly enough, many of the District's residents do not get their water supply from Mugdock and Craigmaddie reservoirs, but rather from Burncrooks reservoir.

GASWORKS AND ELECTRICITY

A private gasworks was built by John Learmont in 1851, just to the east of where the War Memorial now stands in Milngavie. Gas was provided for places as far away as Craigton bleachworks and Craigallian House. However, it was commonly said that if Mr Learmont did not like you, you would not get a gas supply within 100 yards of Milngavie Cross. On April 9, 1901, Milngavie Town Councillors signed a testimonial to John Learmont to mark his jubilee as gas manager. It is said that the Learmonts were frequently invited to dine with those who had a gas supply, and would often be asked "to adjust the pressure of the gas". For this purpose Mr Learmont had a set of light hand tools made, which he took in his carriage when going to dinner with friends.

Bearsden houses were supplied with gas at the end of the 19th century by the Partick, Hillhead and Maryhill Gas Company.

The Strathclyde Electrical Supply Company, later the South of Scotland Electricity Board, and now Scottish Power first installed electricity in the district in what was Scotland's first "garden suburb" in Westerton in 1913. Shortly after the war, the supply was extended to the whole parish.

A private individual had the idea of a water-powered generator in Milngavie. The girders which held the generator can still be seen projecting from the wall on the east side of the Allander, when looking over the wall on the south of the bridge in Douglas Street. The project proved impractical on account of the large rise and fall of the water level.

MINERAL RESOURCES

Quarries, varying in size, but mostly disused, are to be found scattered around the district, from which stone of varying type was extracted. Valuable freestone (sandstone) of a warm creamy colour was quarried at Netherton of Garscube. This was exported to Ireland and the West Indies for public buildings. There was also a good freestone quarry in Baldernock Wood from which attractive building stone was extracted. The old parish church (St Paul's) is built of this stone. In addition there was also quarrying of hard igneous rock at Craigangawn Quarry in the Kilpatrick Hills to the west of the Stockiemuir Road, not far from the site of Auldmurroch Toll and High Craigton. Hard stone was also recently extracted at Craigend quarry, but quarrying is now only active at the Douglas Muir quarry near Crossburn on the Stockiemuir Road, where Tilcon Ltd extract sand

and gravel. Limestone was quarried in the Baljaffray area and elsewhere, and was "burned" using coal mined at Baljaffray up to about 1910. In the 1950s, the National Coal Board made test borings in the Mosshead, Burnbrae and Summerston areas. Coal from a four-foot seam near Mosshead Farm had been used for lime burning. Permission was sought to mine coal at a point east of the Milngavie Road and north of Burnbrae. But this was opposed by Dumbarton County Council on the grounds that the area was scheduled for residential building in stage 1 of the New Kilpatrick Development Plan, by Milngavie Town Council for similar reasons, and by Glasgow Corporation on the grounds that mining would endanger the water pipelines which run through the area. A Secretary of State's inquiry in 1956, lasting over five months, decided against the Coal Board. Thus the area was spared a coal mine in its midst.

MODERN INDUSTRY

From these humble beginnings, industry in the area diversified into a number of smaller businesses, mainly situated in the modern industrial estates at Cloberfield (Bowaters and Flexible Ducting), Riverside (Beaver Skip Services as well as Beaver Kitchens and Bathrooms and the Glasgow Trailer Centre), and Crossveggate (Sandy Carmichael's Handy Hire).

One of the largest factories in the area is Flexible Ducting. Flexible Ducting Ltd, which has a factory at Cloberfield in Milngavie, was registered as a company in 1952. It was during a sales mission in the States the previous year that two directors of a Maryhill rubber fabricating company, Robin and Basil MacLellan, won the confidence of a Connecticut company. The Flexible Tubing Corporation were seeking a licence to make a novel form of flexible ventilations tubing in the UK. On their return, having secured financial backing and the terms of a licence agreed, the new Flexible Ducting Company was set up. In 1953 work began with one employee, Harry Darkins, as works manager and four working directors. By the 21st anniversary of the company in 1974, it was occupying a modern custom-built factory of 80,000 square feet at Cloberfield, employing over 180 people, with an annual production volume of about £2 million, more than half of which was exported. The flexible ducting varies in diameter from a few centimetres to about a metre. It is used in heating and ventilation, for fume and dust removal, for air conditioning in ships, hotels and hospitals, for vacuum cleaners, hair driers and in automobile engines.

ACKNOWLEDGEMENTS

This second edition of "Remains to be Seen" contains basically the same text as that of the First Edition, with slight changes. As a result, my thanks must be extended to the same persons, with a few additions.

Many additional photographs have been added to this edition.

Thanks must be extended to the initial supporters, viz Milngavie & Bearsden Herald, Bearsden and Milngavie Historical Society, and the Milngavie Civic Trust, Dr Grant, Mr McSkimming, Mr Brown, Mr G. Grant, Mrs Main, Prof. Robertson, Mr Foxon, Dr Durant, Dr Keppie, Dr Breeze, Mr McCann, Mr McDonald, Mr Wood, Miss S. Jeffrey, Mrs Dent.

For this edition, thanks must be extended to the Bearsden and Milngavie District Council; Mr Laurie, The Chief Executive, for his determination that this second edition was badly needed; my own library staff, in particular Janice Page for her painstaking typing.

SHEENA V. PETERS, F.L.A.
Chief Librarian
Bearsden and Milngavie District Council

BIBLIOGRAPHY

Bearsden Town Council,
Bearsden, a Guide to
the Burgh 1971

Bearsden Town Council,
The Burgh of Bearsden 1975

MacDonald, Hugh.
Rambles Round Glasgow

**Milngavie and Bearsden Herald
Milngavie Town Council**
The Burgh of Milngavie

Peters, Sheena V.
Milngavie in Old Picture Postcards,
European Library in Zaltbommel,
Netherlands 1983
Bearsden in Old Picture Postcards,
European Library in Zaltbommel,
Netherlands 1983

Roger, David.
Stories of Old Milngavie, Heather
Bank Press Milngavie 1984

Shearer, J.A.
In and Around Milngavie 1908,
1926 and 1930
Editions, D. McLeod, Kirkintilloch

Smith, Guthrie J.
Milngavie and the District,
Sketches Historical and
Topographical Lecture to Milngavie
Mechanics Institution 1878

**The Old Statistical
Account of Scotland 1799
The New Statistical
Account of Scotland 1845
The Third Statistical
Account of Scotland 1959**

PREHISTORY

The Archeological Site and Monuments of Dumbarton District, Clydebank District and Milngavie and Bearsden District, Strathclyde Region Royal Commission on the Ancient and Historical Monuments of Scotland 1978.

THE ROMANS

Breeze, D.J.

The Roman Fort at Bearsden 1973 Excavation – and interim report, Department of the Environment H.M.S.O.
Bearsden Fort, Department of the Environment H.M.S.O.
The Roman Fort on the Antonine Wall at Bearsden, Studies in Scottish Antiquity presented to Stewart Cruden 1984,
John Donald, Edinburgh

Robertson, Anne.

The Antonine Wall 1960; rev. ed., 1973

Johnstone, Anne.

The Wild Frontier, Moubray House Press

Keppie, Lawrence.

Roman Distance Slabs from the Antonine Wall, Hunterian Museum, University of Glasgow.

THE CHURCH

Gardner, W. Reid.

Cairns Church of Scotland 1938

Lees J. Cameron.

The Abbey of Paisley from its foundation to its dissolution, Gardner, Paisley 1878

McCardel, James.

The Parish of New Kilpatrick 1949; New Kilpatrick and its Story 1973

Peat, Rev J.T.

Milngavie and its Parish Church

Scott, Jack.

A Romanesque Censer from Bearsden, Glasgow, Glasgow Archeological Journal 1, 1969, 43-46

THE LAND

Bearsden and Milngavie Historical Society

Local History Group – notes

McPhail, J.M.M.

A Short History of Dunbartonshire 1962

MacKie, J.D.

A History of Scotland, Penguin Books 1978

Napier, Mark.

The Lannox of Auld 1800, David Douglas, Edinburgh

Maclehose, J.

Old Country Houses of Old Glasgow Gentry 1870

Strathclyde Regional Archives

Mains Papers TD 206/1, Garscube Papers
TD 219/23/1/2 23/1/1 23/2

Ure, Rev. David.

General View of Agriculture in the County of Dumbarton 1974

INDUSTRY

Butt, J.

The Industrial Archaeology of Scotland, David and Charles 1968

Clow, A. & N.
The Chemical Revolution,
Batchworth Press 1952

Glasgow Journal,
March 21 April 1 1754

House, Jack.
A Century of Box Making
1850-1950 for Andrew Ritchie
& Son Ltd

Marwick, J.D.
The Water Supply to the
City Published by the
City of Glasgow 1901

Strathclyde Regional Archives,
B10/12/1 171-2, B10/15/5945,
TO 589/636

**Strathclyde Water
Department,**
Water Supply from Loch Katrine
to Glasgow and Environs 1983

TRANSPORT
Cormack, Ian L.
Glasgow Tramways (1973)
Scottish Tramways Museum
Society

Folkard, L.F.
British Trams: A Pictorial Survey
1978

**Johnston,
Colin and Hume, John.**
Glasgow Stations 1979

Oakley, C.A.
The Last Tram 1962, Glasgow
Corporation Transport Department

Thomas, John.
A Regional History of the
Railways of Great Britain, vol VI,
Scotland The Lowlands and the
Borders 1971

MAPS
Pont, Timothy
Map of the Lennox, Amsterdam
1656

Richardson, T.
Map of the Town of Glasgow and
Country Seven Miles Round 1795

Ordnance Survey
1857, 1861, 1895, 1922

---

*Many more items are available for loan as well as consultation from the
Local History Department of Bearsden and Milngavie District Libraries
situated at Brookwood Library, Drymen Road, Bearsden.*

BEARSDEN & MILNGAVIE
Seven Decades Ago

Above: ACADEMY and WAR MEMORIAL
Bearsden

Below: WAR MEMORIAL
Milngavie